Cornerstones of Freedom

The Star-Spangled Banner

Deborah Kent

CHILDRENS PRESS®
CHICAGO

Library of Congress Cataloging-in-Publication Data

Kent, Deborah.
    The star-spangled banner / by Deborah Kent.
        p. cm.—(Cornerstones of freedom)
    Summary: An account of how, during the War of 1812, Francis
Scott Key came to write the poem that became the national anthem.
    ISBN 0-516-06630-7
    1. Key, Francis Scott, 1779–1843. Star-spangled banner—Juvenile
literature. 2. United States—History—War of 1812—Literature and
the war—Juvenile literature. 3. Poets, American—19th century—
Biography—Juvenile literature. 4. Star-spangled banner (Song)—
Juvenile literature. [1. Key, Francis Scott, 1779–1843. 2. Star-
spangled banner (Song) 3. Poets, American. 4. Lawyers.
5. United States—History—War of 1812.] I. Title. II. Series.
PS2167.S73K46 1995
349.73'092—dc20
[B]   95-836
                                                               CIP
                                                                AC

On a sultry afternoon in late August 1814, Dr. William Beanes sat in his garden, enjoying a glass of wine with two of his friends. The United States was at war with Great Britain. Only a few days before, on August 24, British troops had burned Washington, D.C., thirty miles away. But tonight Dr. Beanes and his friends were celebrating. The British army had marched away from Beanes's village of Upper Marlborough, Maryland, leaving its houses and farms unharmed.

During their stay in Upper Marlborough, two British commanders had stationed themselves at Dr. Beanes's house, the finest in the village. Although he was a staunch American patriot, sixty-five-year-old Dr. Beanes had treated the officers courteously while they were under his roof. Now, to his joy, the British soldiers were gone, and Upper Marlborough was left in peace.

A British soldier from the War of 1812

But not all of the British troops had left the village. Suddenly seven young men, stragglers from the main army, burst into the garden. They demanded some of the doctor's wine. Outraged, Dr. Beanes called for help. When several townspeople arrived, the doctor told them to arrest the soldiers for disorderly conduct. One of the soldiers escaped, but the other six men were dragged off to jail. Catching up with the main body of the army, he told his story to the commanders.

Past midnight that night, Dr. Beanes awoke to pounding on his door. A band of British soldiers forced their way into the house and announced that the doctor was under arrest for mistreating British troops. The doctor barely had time to dress, and he left the house without his spectacles. Within minutes, he was riding bareback over thirty-five miles of rough roads to British headquarters at Benedict, Maryland. From there he was taken aboard Admiral Sir Alexander Cochrane's flagship, the *Tonnant*. The doctor was held prisoner in the ship's forecastle.

The arrest of an elderly doctor might have been forgotten as an unimportant detail of the War of 1812. But the arrest began a string of intriguing events that resulted in the creation of America's national anthem, "The Star-Spangled Banner."

Francis Scott Key

Dr. Beanes was one of the leading citizens of Upper Marlborough. When they learned of his arrest, his friends rallied to his support. After discussing the doctor's plight, they turned for help to one of the best lawyers in Washington, thirty-five-year-old Francis Scott Key.

Francis Scott Key had known Dr. Beanes for many years. In fact, he knew most of the prominent people in Maryland and Washington. He and his wife, Mary, loved to entertain. The region's leading lawyers, physicians, poets, and clergymen were frequent guests at the Keys' home in Georgetown, a quiet residential section of the capital. As a lawyer, Key was famous for his eloquence. Juries were easily swayed by his impassioned speeches, enlivened by his poetic turns of phrase.

Francis Scott Key's Georgetown house

Though the law was Key's profession, poetry was his great love. On occasion, he amused his guests by reciting lines he had written himself. If he left his wife a note about household affairs, he sometimes wrote it in humorous verse. One such memo, announcing that guests were expected for dinner, ran:

Mrs. Key will hereby see
That Judges two or three,
And one or two more
So as to make exactly four,
Will dine with her to-day;
And as they cannot stay,
Four o'clock the hour must be
For dinner, and six for tea
And toast and coffee.
So saith her humble servant
F. S. KEY

James Madison (1751–1836) was the fourth president of the United States. He served two four-year terms as president, from 1809 to 1817.

In 1812, hostilities between Great Britain and the young American nation had erupted into full-blown warfare. The War of 1812, as it came to be known, would determine which nation ruled on the high seas. At first, Francis Scott Key opposed the war on religious grounds. A deeply devout man, he believed that war of any kind went against the teachings of the Bible. Yet, when British forces threatened the Maryland coast, Key's attitude changed. In August 1814, he volunteered as an aide to General Walter Smith, commander of the First Brigade of the District Militia.

As soon as he heard about the doctor's situation, Key began his attempt to obtain his friend's release. First Key went to President James Madison, who granted him permission to go to the British fleet under a flag of truce.

Key then gathered letters of testimony from several captured British officers whom Dr. Beanes had treated for wounds after the recent Battle of Bladensburg. One after another, the letters stated that Dr. Beanes had shown them great kindness and compassion, despite the fact that they were enemy soldiers. Finally, Key enlisted the help of his friend, John S. Skinner, who had previously arranged prisoner exchanges. The two men then set sail in a small vessel called a cartel boat. They set out to meet the British fleet in the Chesapeake Bay.

After two days of sailing, Key and Skinner found the fleet of sixteen ships anchored near the mouth of the Patapsco River. Honoring the flag of truce, Admiral Cochrane took them aboard the *Tonnant.* The two Americans noticed immediately that the crew was in a state of excitement. The fleet was preparing to sail. From overheard scraps of conversation, Key and Skinner realized that the British were planning to attack the city of Baltimore, thirteen miles upstream on the Patapsco River.

An official appeal for Beanes's release had arrived earlier, and the British had already reviewed it. On board the *Tonnant,* Key and Skinner dined with the British commanders, and they discussed the matter. The British agreed to set Dr. Beanes free.

But the matter could not be concluded so quickly. The British commanders refused to let Beanes or his rescuers leave immediately. From their short time aboard the ship, the Americans had learned too much about the British attack plans. They would have to stay with the fleet until the battle for Baltimore was over. Beanes, Key, and Skinner would be "guests" of the British on H.M.S. *Surprize*.

A British warship fires on an American city during the War of 1812.

The War of 1812 reached a dire point for the United States when British soldiers captured and burned Washington, D.C.

Exhausted and humiliated by his ordeal, Dr. Beanes was overjoyed to see Key and Skinner. The three men were treated with respect by the *Surprize*'s captain. For several anxious days, they watched the preparations for the coming battle. As the fleet set sail up the Patapsco, the Americans were ordered back into their cartel boat, which was towed by the *Surprize*. Six British marines stood guard over them, so that they could not try to reach shore and raise an alarm.

The people of Baltimore were already bracing themselves for an attack. For days, men, women, and children worked feverishly, digging trenches and building walls of earth to protect the city. The nation's capital, Washington, D.C., had already fallen, and Baltimore must not meet the same fate.

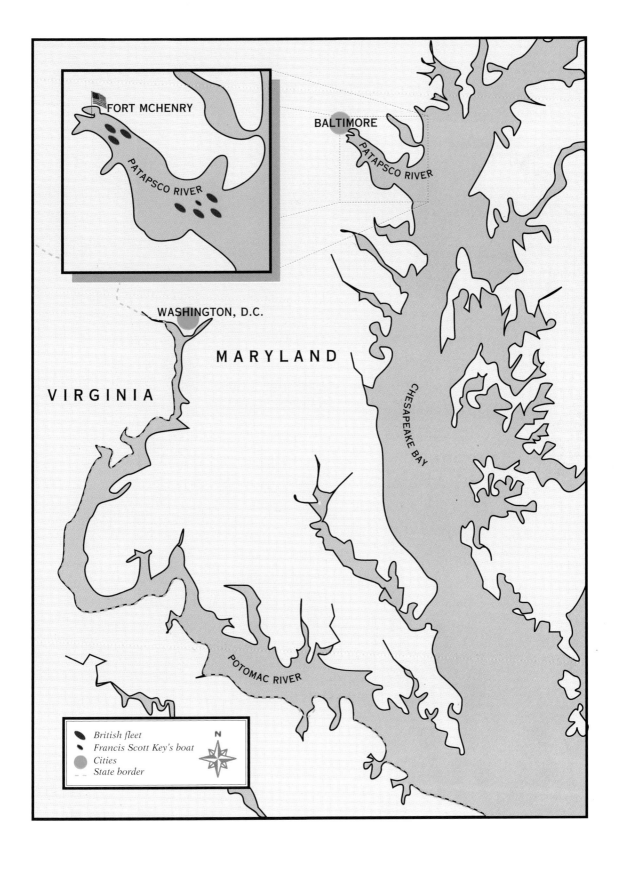

FORT MCHENRY

PATAPSCO RIVER

BALTIMORE

PATAPSCO RIVER

WASHINGTON, D.C.

MARYLAND

VIRGINIA

CHESAPEAKE BAY

POTOMAC RIVER

British fleet
Francis Scott Key's boat
Cities
State border

N

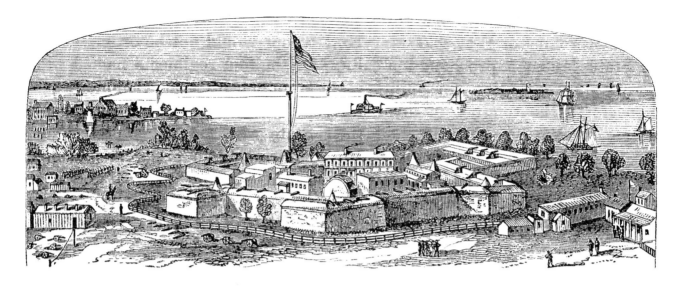

Fort McHenry sat on the shores of the Chesapeake Bay.

Baltimore's chief defense was Fort McHenry, a star-shaped structure of red brick on Whetstone Point in the Patapsco River. Fort McHenry held some one thousand American troops under the command of Lieutenant Colonel George Armistead. A band of militiamen called the Fencibles supported the army troops. The Fencibles were commanded by Key's brother-in-law, Judge Joseph Hopper Nicholson. The fort's "42-pounders" (cannons that could fire forty-two-pound shells) loomed over Chesapeake Bay.

American soldiers from the War of 1812

To block the British fleet from approaching Baltimore too closely, Colonel Armistead ordered twenty-two American ships to be sunk in the Patapsco near the city. The sunken vessels clogged the

waterway, making it impossible for the British fleet to draw near. But the British cannons could fire at long range, so the fort still was not safe.

The British had planned a two-pronged attack on Baltimore. Troops under General Robert Ross would attack the city by land from the north. At the same time, the British fleet would bombard Fort McHenry. Before the land assault began, however, General Ross was killed by an American sniper. Without his leadership, the British land troops fell into confusion and were quickly defeated. For the British, the only hope for victory depended on capturing Fort McHenry.

British general Robert Ross is killed in battle near Baltimore.

At 6:00 A.M. on September 13, the British fleet began to fire on Fort McHenry from about two miles away. Some of the ships sent off rockets that were like tremendous, modern-day firecrackers. They lit the sky with terrifying streaks of flame. Far more lethal were the 200-pound bombs the British cannon hurled at the fort. The bombs were hollow, iron shells packed with gunpowder. When they exploded, they flung deadly, razor-sharp fragments of metal in

British ships in Chesapeake Bay bombard Fort McHenry.

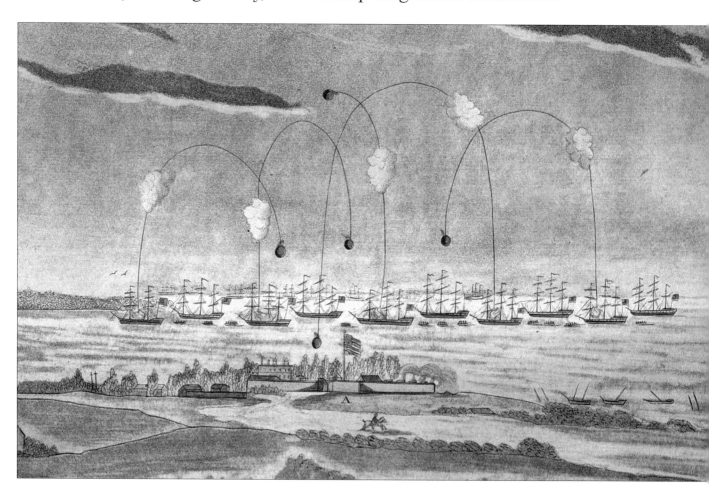

all directions. Because the fleet was firing from such a distance, however, many of these bombs did not reach the fort and burst harmlessly in midair.

From the deck of the cartel boat, Francis Scott Key, John Skinner, and Dr. Beanes were front-row spectators as the battle raged. The deafening roar of the cannons surrounded them. The air was hazy with smoke and pungent with the smell of gunpowder. Key used a small telescope to observe the battle more closely.

Through the smoke, it was difficult to see exactly what was happening at Fort McHenry. But throughout the battle, Key and his companions could see the fort's American flag waving in the breeze. They knew that if the flag was lowered on its staff, the fort had surrendered. But at sunset, the banner still floated high and proud over Fort McHenry.

As night fell, Dr. Beanes retired to the cabin and tried to sleep, despite the din of the fighting. After a time, Skinner, too, went below. But Francis Scott Key could not think of sleep. He worried about the fate of his brother-in-law, Judge Nicholson, and of his other friends in the militia. If the British were victorious, Key feared that they would burn Baltimore as they had burned Washington. Hundreds of civilians might be injured or killed, and thousands of families could be left homeless.

Key remained on deck all night, searching through the smoke and darkness for clues to the battle's outcome. Whenever another rocket streamed across the sky, he caught a reassuring glimpse of the Fort McHenry flag.

At about 1:00 A.M., the firing ceased abruptly. For an hour, the harbor was haunted by a terrifying silence. Key waited tensely, wondering what the strange stillness could mean. Then he realized that the *Surprize* was moving, towing the little cartel boat farther upstream. The fleet was drawing as close as possible to Fort McHenry, in readiness for the final assault.

Key and his party watch the battle from their cartel boat.

Later in the night, the firing began again.
The British bombardment was even more
intense than it had been before. The ships
were still out of range of Fort McHenry's 42-
pounders. But from time to time, the fort sent
off a volley of fire to show that it had no
intention of surrendering.

Toward dawn, the firing ceased abruptly
once more. Beanes and Skinner joined Key on
deck, wondering what had happened. Key
picked up his telescope and strained to see
through the dimness. According to legend, Dr.
Beanes stood at his side, peering about him,
wishing he had his spectacles.

"Can you see the flag?" the doctor asked
again and again. "Is the banner still there?"

As the smoke clears, Key sees the American flag flying above Fort McHenry, and he is inspired to write a poem depicting the moment of victory.

At last the sky brightened with the first morning light. Key gazed through his telescope and uttered a cry of joy. He saw a tremendous new American flag raised over Fort McHenry. The smaller, battle-worn flag was brought down, and the bright new banner of red, white, and blue now waved triumphantly in the breeze.

Suddenly, the opening lines of a poem flooded Key's mind. He pulled an old letter from his pocket and jotted the words hastily on its back. Perhaps Dr. Beanes's question echoed in his ears as he wrote:

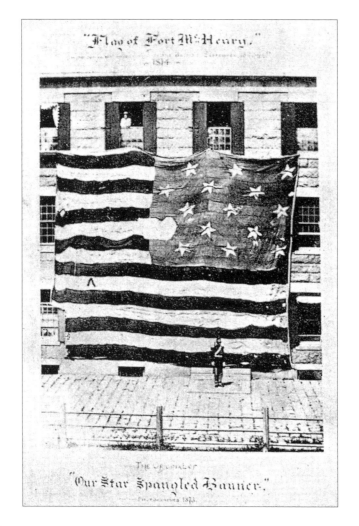

This is the actual flag that was raised above Fort McHenry and inspired Key's poem. It is shown in an 1873 photograph.

Oh say can you see,
by the dawn's early light
What so proudly we hailed,
at the twilight's last gleaming..."

The British had fired about 1,800 bombs at Fort McHenry. But the sunken ships in the river had kept the fleet from coming close enough to do any real harm. In the combined land and sea assaults, only four Americans died and twenty-four were wounded.

Baltimore had resisted capture by the enemy. Now, after twenty-four hours of fighting, the British prepared to make a full retreat. The British defeat at Baltimore was a key to America's eventual victory in the war. The fighting between the United States and Britain ended in 1815.

As the British prepared to leave Baltimore on September 16, 1814, they finally set free Francis Scott Key, John Skinner, and William Beanes. As their cartel boat sailed toward Baltimore, Key continued working on his poem. By the time he reached the city, he had completed four stanzas. In his room at the Indian Queen Hotel, he copied his poem on clean sheets of paper, making only a few small changes as he wrote. This manuscript is now displayed at the Maryland Historical Society.

On September 17, the next morning, Key went to visit his brother-in-law, Judge Nicholson, who had just returned home from Fort McHenry. The two men discussed the battle, and Key showed Nicholson his new poem. He explained how the lines had struck him like a bolt of inspiration. "I felt that I had to write it," he told his brother-in-law. "If it had been a hanging matter to make that poem, I must have made it."

Nicholson was impressed when he read the poem, and he urged Key to have it printed so that copies could be sold. Nicholson set out in search of a printer who could do the job. Most of the newspaper and printing offices in Baltimore were closed because the city was still recovering from the battle. But at one printing office, Nicholson found a fourteen-year-old apprentice named Samuel Sands. The boy assured them that he knew how to set up the type for a "broadside"—a handbill that measured about eight by six inches.

In these first copies, the poem was entitled "Defence of Fort M'Henry." Nicholson wrote a brief introduction, explaining that the poem

A portion of Francis Scott Key's original manuscript of the "Star-Spangled Banner"

The Star-spangled banner.

O say: can you see by the dawn's early light
What so proudly we hail'd at the twilight's last gleaming
Whose broad stripes and bright stars, through the clouds of the fight,
O'er the ramparts we watch'd were so gallantly streaming?
And the rocket's red glare — the bomb bursting in air
Gave proof through the night that our flag was still there?
O say, does that star-spangled banner yet wave
O'er the land of the free & the home of the brave? —

was the creation of an eyewitness to the battle. But Francis Scott Key's name did not appear on the original broadside.

A note at the top of the handbill explained that the poem should be sung to the tune of "To Anacreon in Heaven," a popular melody in both the United States and England. "To Anacreon in Heaven" was composed by John Stafford Smith, an English conductor and organist. Anacreon was an ancient Greek poet whose work celebrated the joys of love and wine. The original lyrics were sung regularly by the Anacreontic Society, a London glee club for men. In the United States, the tune was used as a patriotic song called "Adams and Liberty." Key probably had this melody in mind when he wrote his poem, and it was certainly familiar to the people of Baltimore who bought his broadside.

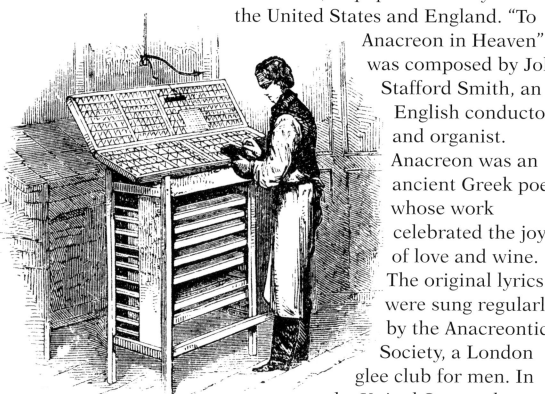

Preparing to print a handbill in an 1800s print shop

Baltimore was jubilant over the British defeat. People sang "Defense of Fort M'Henry" enthusiastically on the streets, in taverns, and on the stage. On September 20, the poem was published in the *Baltimore Patriot,* the first newspaper in the city to reappear after the battle. The editor called the poem a "beautiful and animating effusion," and predicted that it would "long...outlast the occasion, and outlive the impulse, which produced it...."

The Baltimore editor proved correct. Francis Scott Key's song, soon referred to as "The Star-Spangled Banner," remained popular, even as the Fort McHenry battle faded from people's memories. In the 1840s, the song became considered a patriotic "national song," although it did not yet hold the official status as the national anthem. During the Civil War, Union soldiers sang new verses related to the conflict between the North and the South. In 1889, the Secretary of the Navy ordered that the song should be used at all naval flag-raising and flag-lowering ceremonies. In 1903, the U.S. Army decreed that the song should be used for its special occasions. When a band played "The Star-Spangled Banner," soldiers were to stand at attention.

In 1913, Congress opened debate on accepting "The Star-Spangled Banner" as the national anthem of the United States. Many Americans raised objections. Some argued that the song was too difficult due to its wide vocal range. It

John Philip Sousa

had some notes that were very low and some that were very high, which made it difficult for people to sing it and remain in key. Others complained that it was a celebration of militarism and war. Still others objected to the song because the tune came from a drinking song that had been popular in taverns. The *New York Herald Tribune* contended that the song had "words that nobody can remember to a tune that nobody can sing."

Nevertheless, "The Star-Spangled Banner" had thrilled listeners for a century. John Philip Sousa, composer of some of America's most loved patriotic marching tunes, spoke for millions of people when he said, "What

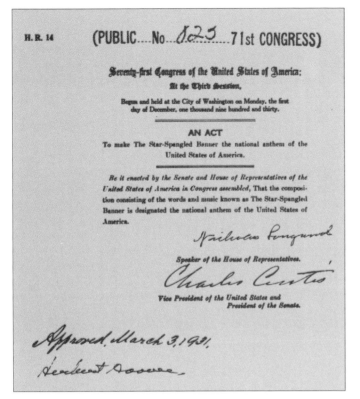

On March 3, 1931, President Herbert Hoover (right) signed Congress's "Star-Spangled Banner" act (left).

matter the words? The spirit is what counts. No true American can fail to be stirred when it is played."

For fifteen years the debate raged on. Then, in 1928, the Veterans of Foreign Wars launched an all-out campaign to have the song adopted. With the aid of more than eighty other patriotic organizations, the VFW collected five million signatures on a petition. The VFW presented the petition to Congress in 1930. Faced with such overwhelming pressure, Congress finally approved the resolution. President Herbert Hoover signed the bill into law on March 3, 1931. On that date, "The Star-Spangled Banner" became the national anthem of the United States.

The enormous flag that inspired the national anthem had an interesting story of its own. In 1813, a year before the battle at Fort McHenry, a Baltimore seamstress named Mary Pickersgill was hired to make two flags for the fort. The first, a small flag called a "storm flag," was flown throughout the battle. Colonel Armistead also asked her to make a much larger flag that would measure approximately thirty feet from top to bottom and forty-two feet in across.

Colonel George Armistead

Mary Pickersgill had learned the art of making flags from her mother, and now she was teaching it to her fourteen-year-old daughter, Caroline. But she had never been asked to make a banner so large! Many years later, as an old woman, Caroline Pickersgill remembered:

The flag being so very large...my mother was obliged to obtain permission from the proprietor of "Claggett's Brewery," which was in our neighborhood, to spread it out in their malt-house, and I remember seeing her down on the floor placing the stars....The flag I think contained four hundred yards of bunting, and my mother worked many nights until 12 o'clock to complete it in a given time.

In 1813, the official flag of the United States had fifteen stripes of alternating red and white, and fifteen white stars on a blue field. The stars represented the fifteen states that had joined the

Union up to that time. Each star in Mary Pickersgill's giant flag measured two feet from tip to tip.

This was the flag that Francis Scott Key saw raised triumphantly above Fort McHenry. After the battle, the flag became the property of Colonel Armistead. One large corner was cut away to wrap the body of a soldier who died defending the fort. The flag was eventually mended, trimmed down, and mounted on a sturdy canvas backing. This "Star-Spangled Banner" is considered one of the nation's treasures, and it now hangs in the Smithsonian Institution in Washington, D.C.

A replica of the fifteen-star American flag that flew above Fort McHenry

In the years after he wrote his famous song, Francis Scott Key continued to distinguish himself as a dedicated public servant. He assisted in the founding of a "recolonization society" to assist freed slaves' return to Africa. Key was a vigorous opponent of the practice of bringing slaves from Africa to the United States.

Many generations are now familiar with Francis Scott Key's "Star-Spangled Banner" as our national anthem. Schoolchildren sing the song all the time (right), and it has become customary for people to sing the anthem before almost every major sporting event (opposite page).

Key was a respected lawyer, and he eventually became attorney general for the District of Columbia. But despite his other accomplishments, he is remembered almost exclusively for the poem he wrote in September 1814, when the rising sun revealed the Stars and Stripes above the walls of Fort McHenry. Few Americans can hear "The Star-Spangled Banner" without thrilling to its stately melody and triumphant words, hoping that the flag will always wave "o'er the land of the free and the home of the brave."

The Star-Spangled Banner
By Francis Scott Key

O say can you see by the dawn's early light,
What so proudly we hailed at the twilight's last gleaming;
Whose broad stripes and bright stars, through the perilous fight,
O'er the ramparts we watched, were so gallantly streaming?
And the rockets' red glare, the bombs bursting in air,
Gave proof through the night that our flag was still there,
  O say, does that star-spangled banner yet wave
  O'er the land of the free and the home of the brave?

On the shore dimly seen through the mists of the deep,
Where the foe's haughty host in dread silence reposes,
What is that which the breeze, o'er the towering steep,
As it fitfully blows, now conceals, now discloses?
Now it catches the gleam of the morning's first beam,
In full glory reflected now shines on the stream,
  'Tis the star-spangled banner—O long may it wave
  O'er the land of the free and the home of the brave!

And where is that band who so vauntingly swore,
That the havoc of war and the battle's confusion
A home and a country should leave us no more?
Their blood has washed out their foul footsteps' pollution.
No refuge could save the hireling and slave
From the terror of flight, or the gloom of the grave,
  And the star-spangled banner in triumph doth wave
  O'er the land of the free and the home of the brave!

Oh! thus be it ever, when freemen shall stand
Between their loved homes and the war's desolation!
Blest with victory and peace, may the heaven-rescued land
Praise the Power that hath made and preserved us a nation.
Then conquer we must, for our cause it is just,
And this be our motto: "In God is our trust,"
  And the star-spangled banner in triumph shall wave
  O'er the land of the free and the home of the brave!

Hillary Rodham Clinton

Garth Brooks

Tommy Lasorda

GLOSSARY

Bombardment

Militia

anthem – a song of praise, honor, or happiness

banner – a flag; a piece of cloth attached to a pole on which a sign or symbol is painted

bombardment – an intense, constant rain of bombs

broadside – a handbill; a sheet of paper with printed text

cartel boat – a small sailing ship; used by Key and Skinner to reach the British fleet in Baltimore Harbor

eloquence – the ability to speak or write beautifully, clearly, or persuasively

flagship – the ship in a fleet carrying the commanding officer and flying his flag

forecastle – rooms below the deck in the bow (front) of a ship

42-pounders – large cannons kept at Fort McHenry that could fire shells weighing forty-two pounds

gunpowder – an explosive powder used in guns and cannons; the explosion of the powder propels a bullet or cannon shell out of the weapon

militia – a group of soldiers

patriot – one who is loyal to his country

seamstress – a person who sews for a living

spangled – covered with many brilliant objects, such as stars

spectacles – eyeglasses

staff – a pole on which a flag is hung

stanza – a grouping of several lines in a poem

truce – a break in battle in which both sides agree to stop firing upon another

twilight – the very dim light in the sky at either sunrise or sunset

TIMELINE

1779 Francis Scott Key born

1812
1813   } War of 1812
1814
1815

August/September:
Beanes arrested by British
soldiers; Key and Skinner
go aboard British fleet to
negotiate Beanes's release

September 13:
British fleet begins attack
of Fort McHenry;
Key watches all night

September 14:
British defeated at
Fort McHenry; Key writes
first verse of poem

September 16:
Key, Skinner, and Beanes set
free by British

September 17:
Key's poem completely written

September 20:
Key's song published in the
Baltimore Patriot

Mary Pickersgill
hired to make
flags for Fort
McHenry

1843 Francis Scott Key dies

1861
         } American Civil War
1865

1889 Secretary of Navy orders "Star-Spangled
        Banner" to be played at flag ceremonies

1913 Congress first debates adopting
        "Banner" as national anthem

1931 *March 3:* President Hoover signs
        bill making "Banner" official
        national anthem

INDEX (**Boldface** *page numbers indicate illustrations.*)

PHOTO CREDITS

Cover, ©Jim Whitmer/Jim and Mary Whitmer; 1, Maryland Historical Society, Baltimore; 2, North Wind Picture Archives; 3, The Bettmann Archive; 5, Stock Montage, Inc.; 6, Culver Pictures, Inc.; 7, Stock Montage, Inc.; 9, 10, 12 (both pictures), North Wind; 13, The Bettmann Archive; 14, Maryland Historical Society, Baltimore; 16, The Bettmann Archive; 17, North Wind; 18, The Bettmann Archive; 19, 21, 22, North Wind; 24, Culver Pictures, Inc.; 25 (left), The Bettmann Archive; 25 (right), 26, Stock Montage, Inc.; 27, ©James Rowan; 28, AP/Wide World; 29 (background), The Bettmann Archive; 29 (top), ©Jonathan Daniel/Allsport USA; 29 (middle), ©Damian Strohmeyer/Allsport USA; 29 (bottom), ©J.D. Cuban/Allsport USA; 30 (top), Maryland Historical Society, Baltimore; 30 (middle), North Wind; 31 (left), The Bettmann Archive; 31 (right), ©James Rowan

ADDITIONAL PICTURE IDENTIFICATIONS

Page 1: *The fighting at Fort McHenry*

Page 2: *British ships blockade Chesapeake Harbor.*

STAFF

Project Editor: Mark Friedman

Design & Electronic Composition: TJS Design

Photo Editor: Jan Izzo

Cornerstones of Freedom Logo: David Cunningham

ABOUT THE AUTHOR

Deborah Kent grew up in Little Falls, New Jersey, and received her B.A. from Oberlin College. She earned a master's degree in social work from Smith College, and worked for four years at the University Settlement House on New York's Lower East Side.

Ms. Kent left social work to begin a career in writing. She published her first novel, *Belonging*, while living in San Miguel de Allende, Mexico. She has written a dozen novels for young adults, as well as numerous nonfiction titles for children. She lives in Chicago with her husband and their daughter, Janna.